Air Fryer Cookbook

Delicious Air Fryer Recipes Made Simple

Contents

Introduction

First off I would like to thank you for downloading this book and being part of the people who have had life changing experiences with what you're about to get into.

What if I were to tell you that eating fries doesn't have to put your health at risk? What if I told you the very same thing for some of your favorite fried foods that you're usually told not to eat? As outrageous as it sounds there is a way you can enjoy your favorite fried foods without adding the extra pounds and there's no other way than with the Airfryer. Since you've picked up this book I'm guessing that you probably have heard about it already so I'll just skip through some of the unnecessary talking and head straight into what this book will do for you.

Created for individuals like you who are looking for a healthier alternative, this book will provide you with all the information that you need to know on Airfryers. From basic definitions to numerous must try recipes. But you get so much more than just that from this book. This book also highlights some of the best Airfryers on the market and equips you with the information that you need to purchase the right Airfryer that's best suited for you. What's the point in having delicious recipes if you haven't got the right Airfryer to match? If you're thinking of bettering your health then what better way to start than by eating healthier versions of your favorite meals?

We all know how difficult it is to start a new diet that limits your choices of food but why start there and place that much pressure on yourself when you can start with a healthy alternative like an Airfryer, making life much easier. If you want to know more about Airfryer cooking then here's your chance. Take it!

Chapter 1: Air Fryer Overview

We all love fast food, right? You know, the slightly salted French fries, mouthwatering crispy chicken, lightly browned buttery biscuits and so on. But what's wrong with meals such as those. It can't be the taste that's for sure, then what it is? Ah yes, they're considered to be unhealthy and contain enormous amounts of calories per serving. Sigh, if only there was a way to enjoy foods such as those without all the health risk involved. You probably saw this coming but there is and it can be done with the use of an air fryer.

What is an air fryer you ask? First off I'll let you know it's one of the best inventions ever created for the kitchen in terms of cooking/frying foods. Air fryers are kitchen appliances that uses superheated air of up to 390*F (200*C) to fry foods such as fries, chicken, potato chips and practically anything that needs frying. The air fryer is designed to circulate hot air around the food cooking it in a way similar to if it were to be fried in a deep fryer. The only thing different is that this method of frying food is many times healthier than deep frying, plus there's more benefits to air fryer cooking that will be discussed later on.

Now, if this is new to you a few questions might have popped up in your head but don't worry, they all will be answered in a matter of a few pages read. One thing which seems to always be of concern to anyone trying this for the very first time is, are they able to get some of the same pleasures of traditional recipes? This simply means does the food taste the same and has other similar features to traditional recipes such as texture, smell, appearance, etc. Fortunately this is an area which was studied by professor Shaker, M. Arafat which the results were later published by the Journal of Food and Nutrition Sciences. The study compared the air fryer method of cooking and the traditional way of cooking using French fries and found that the air fryer method did better than the traditional in the following areas:

- Taste
- Color
- Smell
- Hardness
- Crispiness
- Oiliness

The only area which the air fryer method of cooking could not surpass the traditional method was in appearance. Although the air fryer wasn't able to get 7/7, I think 6/7 is still pretty good, don't you?

BENEFITS OF AN AIR FRYER

Healthier Dishes

As mentioned before one of the great features of an air fryer is that it allows you to cook healthier meals without sacrificing your favorite foods. Foods cooked with air fryers contain up to 80% less fat than other fryers that are available on the market. No, it's not a typo! Up to 80% less fat which means that you're not taking in any unwanted substances and are supporting good health by using air fryers to prepare meals. No more excess calories or saturated fat to hold you back from looking your best.

Versatile

Another common question with the air fryer is, can it only be used to fry? And that's a really good question because although it's great for cutting away a few pounds when frying you would most like want it to be more than just that. To answer the question, no – the air fryer actually does more than just fry foods and can be used to grill, bake and roast foods. Pretty sweet right? Think of the air fryer as an all-in-one kitchen appliance making it perfect for anyone who loves delicious healthy cooking.

Time Saver

In today's age everyone is on the move and we just don't have the time that we use to like before and that's understandable which is why the air fryer will come in handy for quick and easy to prepare meals. If you're constantly busy you might not have an hour or two to cook on a daily basis but with this appliance the cooking happens quicker than you may think. In only 12 minutes you can be relaxed adding ketchup to your French fries and enjoying healthy, warm French fries.

Air Filter

One thing which I know for a fact that irritates when frying foods is having yourself, the entire kitchen or even majority of the house smelling like what you're cooking. With the air fryer, some come with a built in air filter that eliminates all the unwanted odors that come with frying. No need to grab the air freshener once you're done frying.

Simple Clean up

Cleaning up must be the one area where everyone would agree to be the most hassle with cooking. Whether you're an adult or child cleaning up after meals will always feel like a chore but that doesn't mean it can't be made simpler. In the case of air fryers this pat is the simplest clean up you will have. Designed with this in mind air fryers are made from a non-stick material that prevents foods from sticking to the surface of the appliance. Air fryers are also dishwasher friendly so parts such as the basket, grill and pan can be placed in the dishwasher making cleaning up as mentioned earlier, simple. Although it is recommended to soak the appliance's parts in water before cleaning.

Multiple Meals at Once

This may not have been your first concern but nonetheless it still needs to be addressed. Some air fryers come with the feature of being able to cook more than one food at a time which in my opinion is a great feature. Why wait for one food to be cooked before adding another? Food separators are perfect for cooking more than one food at a time cutting the time taken to cook by almost half.

Inexpensive

Compared to other fryers on the market air fryers are on another level. Not only in what they're capable of doing in terms of being able to grill, roast, fry and bake but also what they may mean to an individual's health. If you were to look at the pros and cons of air fryers you would observe that the pros outweigh the cons by more than just a considerable amount. The value that an air fryer provides is much greater than what it is sold at making this a no brainer for most.

Chapter 2:

Air Fryer Breakfast
Recipes

French Toast Sticks

INGREDIENTS

4 pieces of sliced bread

2 Tbsp soft butter/margarine

2 eggs

Salt

Cinnamon

1 pinch Nutmeg

1 pinch Ground cloves

Icing sugar/maple syrup

Directions

1. Preheat the Airfryer to 360*F (180*C).

2. Crack open 2 eggs into a bowl and add the following ingredients: a pinch of nutmeg and cloves, a dash of salt and cinnamon. Lightly beat the mixture together until well combined.

3. Using the butter or margarine coat each side of the bread with whichever chosen and cut into even strips.

4. Dip each strip into the egg mixture and arrange in the Airfryer to cook.

5. After 2 minutes, remove the pan and spray each side of the bread with cooking spray and return to the Airfryer to be cooked for an additional 4 minutes (check halfway through ensuring that the bread doesn't burn).

6. After the 4 minutes has past or until the egg is cooked and the bread takes on a golden brown color remove from the Airfryer and serve with either a drizzle of icing sugar or maple syrup.

Sugary Cinnamon Doughnuts

INGREDIENTS

2 tbsp butter (at room temperature)

½ cup sugar

2 ¼ cup plain flour

1 ½ tsp baking powder

1 tsp salt

2 large egg yolks

½ cup sour cream

1 ¾ oz (50g) butter (melted)

1/3 cup caster sugar

1 tsp cinnamon

Directions

1. In a bowl add the butter and sugar then press together until crumbly. Add the egg yolks right after and stir until well mixed.

2. In a separate bowl (a second bowl), add in 1/3 of flour as well as ¼ or half of the sour cream and mix.

3. When mixed follow this by adding another 1/3 of flour and the remaining sour cream and mix once more until well combined. Place the mixture in the fridge while you move on to the next step.

4. Evenly coat the bench with flour and roll-out the dough to be 1cm in thickness. Cut large circles in the dough followed by smaller circles at the center to create the pit of the doughnut.

5. Preheat the Airfryer to 360*F (180*C).

6. Dip a brush into the melted butter and add a thin coat on each side of the doughnut. Add the doughnut to the fryer and allow cooking for approximately 8 minutes.

7. Once cooked remove from the pan and add another layer of butter to the doughnut and immediately dip into the sour cream mixture.

8. Serve hot and enjoy!

Cheesy Garlic Doughnuts

INGREDIENTS

2 dinner rolls

½ cup grated cheese

2 tbsp butter (melted)

Garlic bread seasoning mix

Directions

1. Cut the bread rolls top down, add 2 vertical and 2 horizontal lines across the bread similar to a naughts and crosses style. Ensure that the cut is deep but do not allow the bread to be cut all the way through.

2. Fill the trenches of the bread with grated cheese.

3. Preheat the Airfryer to 360*F (180*C).

4. Add a layer of melted butter onto the top of the rolls and sprinkle over with garlic seasoning.

5. Place the cheese filled rolls in the preheated Airfryer and cook for approximately 5 minutes or until the cheese is melted and the rolls takes on a browned color.

Cranberry Breakfast Muffin

INGREDIENTS

2 ½ oz (75 g) flour

1½ tsp baking powder

1 tsp cinnamon

3 tbsp sugar

1 small egg

75 ml milk

1 ¾ oz (50 g) butter (melted)

2 ½ oz (75 g) dried cranberries

8 paper muffin cups

Directions

1. Preheat the Airfryer to 390*F (200*C). Add within each paper cup another so that there will be a total of 4 paper cups.

2. In a bowl mix well the following ingredients: flour, baking powder, cinnamon, sugar and a pinch of salt.

3. In a second bowl add the milk, egg and melted butter and lightly beat so that the ingredients will be well mixed. Pour the contents of the second bowl into the first and stir adding in the cranberries and mixing them all.

4. Once mixed and the batter is ready spoon it into the doubled muffin cups and add each in the basket of the Airfryer.

5. Bake the muffins for about 15 minutes in the Airfryer or until they become golden brown. When done remove from the Airfryer, let cool then serve and enjoy.

Puff Pastry Bites

INGREDIENTS

7 oz (200 g) ready-made (frozen or chilled) puff
pastry

Filling as desired

2 tbsp milk

Directions

1. Preheat the Airfryer to 390*F (200*C).

2. Into 5x5 cm squares cut 16 squares of pastry
   and spoon the filling onto each square.

3. Hold one corner of the square and fold it over
   the other so that the pastry forms a triangle.
   Wet the edges of the pastry and use a fork to
   press down on the edges to seal.

4. Using a brush coat the pastries with milk and
   add 8 to the Airfryer and bake for about 10
   minutes or until the pastries are golden brown.

5. Repeat the same process for the next few pastries and when done serve and enjoy!

Breakfast Soufflé

INGREDIENTS

2 eggs

2 tbsp (light) cream

Red chili pepper, chopped

Parsley, chopped

Directions

1. Preheat the Airfryer to 390*F (200*C).

2. Add all the ingredients to a bowl and mix well.

3. Transfer to ramekins filing them up halfway with the egg mixture.

4. Add to the Airfryer and bake for about 8 minutes but if you're looking for a softer result (baveux) bake for about 5 minutes.

5. When done let cool, serve and enjoy!

Brazilian Cheese Bread

INGREDIENTS

1 lb (500 g) tapioca flour

5 oz (150 g) milk

3 ½ oz (100 g) Canola or sunflower oil

1 tbsp salt

2 eggs

9 oz (250 g) strong grated cheese

Directions

1. Preheat the Airfryer to 330*F (160*C).

2. Add the following ingredients to a pan: milk, cheese, egg and oil and bring to just below the boiling point stirring constantly.

3. In a bowl add the flour and salt then add the warm milk mixture kneading to form dough.

4. Cut the dough into small even pieces and shape them to form small balls and bake them in the Airfryer for about 13 minutes.

5. When done let cool, serve and enjoy!

Chapter 3

Air Fryer Lunches and Dinners Recipes

Easy Spring Rolls

INGREDIENTS

1 ¾ oz (50g) Asian noodles

1 tablespoon sesame oil

7 oz (200g) mince

1 small onion diced

3 cloves garlic, crushed

1 cup mixed vegetables, fresh or frozen

1 tsp soy sauce

1 packet spring rolls

2 tbsp cold water

Directions

1. Immerse the noodles in hot water and allow them to soak until they soften. Then drain and slice into small lengths.

2. Heat the oil in a skillet and add the following ingredients: diced onion, garlic, mince and mixed vegetables. Cook until the onion softens

and the mince is almost cooked then add the soy sauce.

3. Remove from the pan and add to the noodles stirring the ingredients in a bowl until well combined. Let stand afterwards so that the noodles can absorb the juices.

4. Spread out the spring roll sheets on a flat surface and add strips of the filling across the sheets diagonally. Fold in the top corners and then the sides. On the last fold seal by passing a wet brush over the fold.

5. Preheat the Airfryer to 360*F (180*C).

6. Using vegetable oil add a coat to the spring rolls.

7. Add the spring rolls to the Airfryer and cook for approximately 8 minutes. Repeat until all spring rolls are cooked.

Air Fried Potato Wedges

INGREDIENTS

2 large potatoes

1 tbsp vegetable oil

Sour cream, as required

Sweet chilli sauce, as required

Directions

1. Begin by cutting the potatoes into strips of 8 or 12. Ensure that the sizes are similar in order to be consistent when cooking.

2. Preheat the Airfryer to 360*F (180*C).

3. Add the potatoes in a bag and pour in the oil. Shake the bag so that the potatoes are well coated with a thin layer of oil on them.

4. Place the potatoes into the Airfryer and allow cooking for approximately 15 minutes. When done toss the potatoes and cook for an additional 10 minutes. If the potatoes are still

thick after the final time allow an extra couple minutes of cooking.

5. Serve hot with the sweet chilli sauce and sour cream.

Spicy Country Fries

INGREDIENTS

1 ¾ lbs (800 g) waxy potatoes

2 small, dried chilies or 1 heaped tsp freshly
ground, dried chili flakes

½ tbsp freshly ground black pepper

1 tbsp olive oil

Directions

1. Preheat the Airfryer to 360*F (180*C).

2. Clean the potatoes under running water,
    scrubbing them thoroughly. When done slice
    them into strips of 1 ½ cm.

3. Immerse the fries in a bowl or container of
    water and leave to soak for about 30 minutes.
    Drain once done and pat them dry with a
    kitchen towel.

4. Crush the chilies so that they're fine and add
    them in a bowl with the following ingredients:

curry powder, olive oil and pepper. Mix the ingredients together.

5. Add a coat of the chili mixture to the fries and add them to the Airfryer to be fried for 20 minutes. Remove after the fries takes on a golden brown color but be sure to turn the fries over every now and then while it's frying.

6. Serve on a plate with a pinch of salt and or a side dish.

Grilled Fish Fillets with Pesto Sauce

INGREDIENTS

3 – 7 oz (200g) white fish fillets

1 tbsp olive oil

Pepper & salt

1 bunch fresh basil

2 garlic cloves

2 tbsp pinenuts

1 tbsp grated parmesan cheese

250 ml extra virgin olive oil

Directions

1. Preheat the Airfryer to 360*F (180*C).

2. Using a brush add a coat of olive oil on the fish fillets and season with salt and pepper.

3. Place the fillets in the Airfryer's basket and cook for 8 minutes.

4. In the meantime add the following ingredients into a food processor: basil leaves, garlic, parmesan cheese, pinenuts and olive oil. Pulse or grind the ingredients until it forms a smooth pesto sauce. When done add salt to taste.

5. Remove the fillets from the Airfryer and serve it on a plate topped with the pesto sauce.

Ratatouille

INGREDIENTS

7 oz (200 g) zucchini and/or eggplant

1 yellow bell pepper

2 tomatoes

1 onion, peeled

1 clove garlic, crushed

2 tsp dried Provençal herbs

Freshly ground black pepper

1 tbsp olive oil

Small, round baking dish, 16 cm diameter

Directions

1. Preheat the Airfryer to 390*F (200*C).

2. Cut the following ingredients into 2 cm cubes: zucchini, eggplant, bell pepper, tomatoes, and onion.

3. Add the cubed vegetables to a large bowl and mix in with the garlic, provençal herbs, and half a tsp of salt and pepper to taste.

4. Drizzle olive oil over the vegetables and place it in the Airfryer's basket and cook for about 15 minutes. Half way through the cooking time stir the vegetables once and leave to continue cooking.

5. Serve the ratatouille with fried meat such as entrecôte, or a cutlet.

Crispy Air Fried Tofu

INGREDIENTS

12 oz (350 g) Low-fat Extra Firm Tofu

1 tsp Duck Fat

1 tsp Sesame Oil

1 tsp Maggi

1 tbsp Coriander Paste (optional)

2 tbsp Fish Sauce

2 tbsp Low-sodium Soy Sauce

Directions

1. Begin by cutting the tofu into 1 inch cubes and place in a large bowl to be used for later.

2. Create a marinade by combining all ingredients from the 3rd on the list (sesame oil) downward to the final. If you're using a basket type air fryer microwave the duck fat and mix it into the rest of the marinade ingredients.

3. Pour the marinade over the tofu cubes and let marinade for approximately 30 minutes, tossing a few times in between.

4. In the case of an air fryer which has an air frying pan, melt the duck fat, add the tofu cubes and cook for about 20 minutes, more if you prefer crispier results.

5. In the case of an Airfryer which has a basket cook the tofu at 360*F (180*C) and with the same time span, shaking or tossing the tofu every 10 minutes or so.

Air Fried Burgers

INGREDIENTS

1 pound uncooked 93% extra-lean ground beef

1 tbsp Worcestershire sauce

1 tsp Maggi seasoning sauce

Few drops liquid smoke

½ tsp garlic powder

½ tsp onion powder

½ tsp salt substitute

½ tsp ground black pepper

½ tsp dried oregano

1 tsp dried parsley

Directions

1. This recipe is best prepared with an Actifry but an Airfryer containing a basket can still be used. Just follow the steps accordingly.

2. Using cooking spray, add a coat to the upper part of the Actifry tray and leave for later.

3. In a bowl combine all the ingredients beginning with the Worcestershire sauce down to the final ingredient on the list.

4. In a second larger bowl add the beef and the seasoning mixture as well. Mix the two but be sure not to overwork the meat as it will cause the burgers to be a lot tougher than what it needs to be.

5. Separate the large bulk of meat into 4 patties adding a dent with the thumb at the centre of each patty to prevent the burger from bunching up at the center.

6. Spray the top of each patty lightly and add it to the Actifry.

7. Cook in the Actifry for about 10 minutes with no need to flip the patties.

8. Serve by adding it to a bun as well as any side dish of your choice and enjoy!

Spicy Drumsticks with Barbeque Marinade

INGREDIENTS

4 Chicken drumsticks

1 clove garlic (crushed)

½ tbsp mustard

2 tsp brown sugar

1 tsp chili powder

Freshly ground black pepper

1 tbsp olive oil

Directions

1. Preheat the Airfryer to 390*F (200*C).

2. In a bowl mix in the ingredients for the marinade which includes the following: mustard, brown sugar, chili powder, olive oil, pinch of salt, crushed garlic cloves and freshly ground black pepper to taste.

3. Immerse the drumstick in the marinade ensuring that the drumstick is fully coated with the marinade and leave for 20 minutes.

4. When done remove the drumsticks from the marinade and place it onto the basket and set to roast in the Airfryer for 10 minutes. At that point the drumstick should have taken a brown color.

5. After the first 10 minutes of cooking lower the heat to 300*F (150*C) and roast for an additional 10 minutes.

6. Once done serve with any other dish such as a side of salad and or French bread.

Jerk Chicken Wings

INGREDIENTS

3 lbs chicken wings

2 tbsp olive oil

2 tbsp soy sauce

6 cloves garlic, finely chopped

1 habanero pepper

1 tbsp allspice

1 tsp cinnamon

1 tsp cayenne pepper

1 tsp white pepper

1 tsp salt

2 tbsp brown sugar

1 tbsp fresh thyme, finely chopped

1 tbsp fresh ginger, grated

4 scallions, finely chopped

5 tbsp lime juice

½ cup red wine vinegar

Directions

1. Begin by combining all the ingredients in a large mixing bowl or container and completely immersing the chicken within.

2. Transfer the contents of the bowl to a large enough re-sealable bag (1 gallon bag should do) and place in the fridge for 2 – 24 hours so that the chicken can absorb all the juices.

3. After the wings have been marinated preheat the Airfryer to 390*F (200*C). Remove the chicken from the bag and pat them dry with a paper towel.

4. Add half of the batch of wings to the preheated Airfryer and allow cooking for 14 – 16 minutes. Shake the wings up half way through the cooking process and monitor to not overcook the wings.

5. When done let cool for a couple minutes and serve with a dipping sauce of your choice.

Roasted Vegetables

INGREDIENTS

1 1/3 cup parsnips (1 small), peeled and diced

1 1/3 cup celery (3-4 stalks), peeled and diced

2 red onions cut into wedges

1 1/3 cup butternut squash (1 small), halved, deseeded and cubed

1 tbsp fresh thyme needles

1 tbsp olive oil

Pepper & salt to taste

Directions

1. Preheat the Airfryer to 390*F (200*C).

2. Begin by mixing the cut vegetables (parsnips, celery, onions, butternut squash) together with the thyme and the olive oil in a bowl, then season to taste.

3. Add the vegetables to the Airfryer and roast for about 20 minutes. When done the vegetables

should be nicely browned. Stir the vegetables halfway through the cooking process so that it's well roasted.

4. Serve almost immediately after and enjoy!

Steak Tartare Burgers with Ham

INGREDIENTS

14 oz (400 g) finely minced beef

5 cm white of 1 leek, very finely chopped

1 ¾ oz (50 g) ham, in fine strips

3 tbsp bread crumbs

Freshly ground pepper to taste

Salt to taste

Nutmeg

Directions

1. Preheat the Airfryer to 390*F (200*C).

2. In a large bowl mix the following ingredients: minced beef, bread crumbs, chopped leek, ham, nutmeg and salt and pepper to taste.

3. Knead so that the ingredients are all well combined.

4. Separate the kneaded beef into 4 equal parts and wet your hands to form smooth burgers.

5. Add the burgers to the Airfryer and cook them for about 8 minutes or until nicely browned.

6. Serve the burger with a side of veggies or place between two buns and enjoy!

Fried Meatballs in Tomato Sauce

INGREDIENTS

1 small onion, finely chopped

¾ pounds (12oz) ground beef

1 tbsp chopped fresh parsley

½ tbsp chopped fresh thyme leaves

1 egg

3 tbsp breadcrumbs

Pepper & salt to taste

Directions

1. Preheat the Airfryer to 390*F (200*C).

2. Add all the ingredients into a large bowl and mix them all together.

3. Separate the contents of the bowl into 10 – 12 equal parts and roll each into little balls.

4. Add the meatballs to the Airfryer and set to cook for approximately 8 minutes.

5. When done remove the meatballs and transfer them to an oven dish. Add in the tomato sauce and add the dish back into the Airfryer for an additional 5 minutes at 330*F (165*C) to allow the ingredients to cook through.

6. When cooked remove, serve and enjoy!

Korean BBQ Satay

INGREDIENTS

¾ pound (12 oz) boneless skinless chicken tenders

½ cup low sodium soy sauce

½ cup pineapple juice

¼ cup sesame oil

4 garlic cloves, chopped

4 scallions, chopped

1 tablespoon fresh ginger, grated

2 teaspoons sesame seeds, toasted

1 pinch black pepper

Directions

1. Trim the excess fat and meat off of the chicken by skewering each chicken tender.

2. Add all the other ingredients to a mixing bowl and mix well adding in the skewered chicken and immersing completely in the mixture.

3. Cover the bowl and add to the fridge for 2 – 24 hours.

4. Preheat the Airfryer to 390*F (200*C) after being refrigerated.

5. Pat the chicken dry with a paper towel and add the skewered chicken to the Airfryer for 5 – 7 minutes to be cooked.

6. Remove when cooked, serve and enjoy!

Chimichurri Skirt Steak

INGREDIENTS

1 lb skirt steak

1 cup parsley, finely chopped

¼ cup mint, finely chopped

2 tbsp oregano, finely chopped

3 garlic cloves, finely chopped

1 tsp crushed red pepper

1 tbsp ground cumin

1 tsp cayenne pepper

2 tsp smoked paprika

1 tsp salt

¼ tsp black pepper

¾ cup olive oil

3 tbsp red wine vinegar

Directions

1. Begin by adding all the ingredients besides the steak in a mixing bowl to make the chimichurri.

2. Combine well and add the steak along with ¼ cup of the chimichurri to a re-sealable bag. Cut the steak into two 8 oz pieces for this.

3. Refrigerate overnight and remove 30 minutes prior to cooking.

4. Preheat the Airfryer to 390*F (200*C).

5. Pat the steak dry with a paper towel and add to the Airfryer for 8 – 10 minutes to be cooked for medium rare.

6. When done garnish the steak with 2 tbsp of chimichurri then serve and enoy!

Roast Potatoes with Tuna

INGREDIENTS

4 starchy potatoes, approximately 125 g each

½ tbsp olive oil

1 can of tuna in oil, drained

2 tbsp (Greek) yoghurt

1 tsp chili powder

1 green onion, finely sliced into rings

Freshly ground black pepper

1 tbsp capers

Directions

1. Preheat the Airfryer to 360*F (180*C).

2. Immerse the potatoes in water and allow them to soak for about 30 minutes. When done pat the dry with a kitchen towel.

3. Using a brush give the potatoes a light coat of olive oil and place it in the Airfryer for 30

minutes to fry until crunchy and properly cooked.

4. Add the tuna to a bowl and combine with the chili powder as well as the yoghurt. Stir the ingredients together ensuring that the tuna is mashed up and follow by adding half of the green onion. Season with salt and pepper to taste.

5. Separate the potatoes between 2 plates and slice each in half lengthwise. Create an opening in the potato halves by pushing down at the center and once created fill with the tuna mixture.

6. Finally spoon the capers onto the top of the tuna filling and drizzle with chili powder. Also add the rest of the green onions onto the filling.

7. If interested this can be served with a fresh salad on the side.

Lamb Chops with Garlic Sauce

INGREDIENTS

8 lamb chops

1 garlic bulb

3 tbsp olive oil

1 tbsp fresh oregano, finely chopped

Sea salt to taste

Freshly ground black pepper

Directions

1. Preheat the Airfryer to 360*F (180*C).

2. Add a thin layer of olive oil onto the garlic bulb and place in the Airfryer to be roasted for 12 minutes.

3. In the meanwhile add the following ingredients in a small bowl and mix: freshly chopped oregano, olive oil, sea salt and pepper.

4. Using the herb mixture just made brush half a tablespoon onto the lamb chops and allow to stand for 5 minutes.

5. At this point the garlic should be done or there about so remove it from the Airfryer and preheat once more at 390*F (200*C).

6. Place the lamb chops in the Airfryer's basket and roast for 5-7 minutes or until the lamb chops takes on a nicely browned color. The inside of the lamb maybe somewhat pink but do the same with the other lamb chops until complete.

7. Placing the garlic cloves between the index finger and the thumb squeeze the cloves over the herb oil extracting the juice from it. Mix well with salt and pepper.

8. Drizzle the lamb chops with the garlic sauce and or serve with either couscous or rice.

Pork Tenderloin with Bell Pepper

INGREDIENTS

1 red or yellow bell pepper, in thin strips

1 red onion, in thin slices

2 tsp Provencal herbs

Freshly ground black pepper

1 tbsp olive oil

1 pork tenderloin – 10 oz (300 g)

½ tbsp mustard

Round 15 cm oven dish

Directions

1. Preheat the Airfryer to 360*F (180*C).

2. In the dish mix the following ingredients together: strips of bell pepper, onion, Provencal herbs and to taste salt and pepper.

When mixed add ½ tbsp of olive oil to the dish of vegetables.

3. Slice the pork tenderloin into 4 pieces and season with salt, pepper and mustard by rubbing the pieces of pork thoroughly.

4. Add a coat of olive oil to the pieces of pork as well and place each at the top of the vegetables in the dish.

5. Place the dish in the Airfryer's basket and cook in the Airfryer for 15 minutes roasting the meat and vegetables.

6. Halfway through the roasting flip the meat over and mix the vegetables. When done serve on a plate with a side of salad and or mash potatoes and enjoy.

Crispy Fried Spring Rolls

INGREDIENTS

4 oz (120 g) cooked chicken breast

8 spring roll wrappers

1 celery stalk

1 oz (30 g) carrot

1 oz (30 g) mushrooms

½ tsp finely chopped ginger

1 tsp sugar

1 tsp chicken stock powder

1 egg

1 tsp corn starch

Directions

1. Cut the mushrooms, carrots and celery into long thin strips and add them to a bowl.

2. Shred the chicken breasts apart and add the torn chicken into the bowl with the vegetables as well.

3. Mix the contents of the bowl and add in the ginger, chicken stock powder and sugar. Continue stirring combining the contents to create the filling for the spring rolls.

4. In a separate bowl whisk the egg adding in the corn starch and creating a thick paste through mixing. Set aside when done.

5. Preheat the Airfryer to 390*F (200*C).

6. Lay the spring roll wrappers on a flat surface and add in the chicken filling onto each. Roll the wrappers and using the egg mixture seal the wrappers by adding a coat. Also brush the rolls with oil for a crispy effect.

7. Place the spring rolls in the Airfryer and cook for about 4 minutes.

8. When done remove from the Airfryer's basket and serve on a plate with sweet chili sauce and enjoy!

Cheese-steak Egg Rolls

INGREDIENTS

1 Green Bell Pepper (diced)

1 Medium White Onion (diced)

½ Pound of Cheese of your choice (diced)

2 Packages of Frozen Sliced Steak

1 Package Egg Roll Wrappers

Directions

1. Set a skillet on a medium high heat and add in the diced vegetables. Sauté the onion and the green pepper until they're softened but somewhat crispy. When done remove from the skillet and let cool in a large bowl.

2. Using the same skillet the vegetables were cooked in throw in the steak slices and cook until the pink in the steak has nearly completely faded away. Cook 2 planks of steaks at a time. As the steak slices cook break them apart into bite sized pieces with the spatula.

3. When done add the steak to a paper towel plate so that the towel will capture the excess oil from the steak.

4. After the steak has cooled and oil absorbed by the towel combine the cheese and steak with the veggies. Ensure that everything is well mixed.

5. Lay the wrappers onto a flat surface and add some of the filling (1/4 cup) onto the wrapper so that it fits diagonally on the wrapper.

6. Grab the first corner of the wrap and fold it in. Do the same to the opposite corners that haven't been folded yet and roll the egg roll wrapper over the last corner of the wrap.

7. Place the egg roll wraps in the Airfryer and cook for 10 minutes at 360*F (180*C). After that time is done increase the heat to 390*F (200*C) for an additional 3 minutes. This is to get the right crispiness from the rolls.

8. Let cool for a few minutes when done and enjoy!

Fish and Chips

INGREDIENTS

7 oz (200 g) white fish filet (tilapia, cod, pollack)

1 oz (30 g) tortilla chips

1 egg

10 oz (300 g) red potatoes

1 tbsp vegetable oil

½ tbsp lemon juice

Directions

1. Preheat the Airfryer to 360*F (180*C).

2. Slice the fish into 4 equal pieces and season with salt and pepper. Using the lemon juice rub the fish pieces and leave to sit for 5 minutes.

3. In the meanwhile add the tortilla chips to the food processor and grind until it becomes very fine. Transfer the grinded tortilla in a plate and set aside.

4. Beat the egg in a deep dish and dip each of the fish pieces in adding a coat of the egg. Follow this by covering each piece of fish in the grinded tortilla. Ensure that each piece is fully covered.

5. Scrub the potatoes under running water and when clean cut into thin strips, lengthwise. Immerse the potato strips in a bowl or container of water and soak for at least 30 minutes. When done drain and pat them dry with a kitchen towel. Follow this with a coat of vegetable oil in a bowl.

6. Use the separator to cook the potato strips and fish pieces simultaneously. Insert the separator into the Airfryer and add the fish on one side and the potato on the other.

7. Cook in the Airfryer for 12 minutes and remove when done. Both the fish and the potato strips should now be crispy and have a brown color.

8. Serve on a plate and enjoy!

Salmon Croquettes

INGREDIENTS

1 tin of red salmon (approx. 7 oz/200 g), drained

1 egg, lightly beaten

1 tbsp fresh dill, finely chopped

2 tbsp chives, finely chopped

Freshly ground pepper

1 ¾ oz (50 g) bread crumbs

Directions

1. Preheat the Airfryer to 390*F (200*C).

2. Mash up the salmon in a deep dish. To do this you can use a fork. When done mix the egg and herbs in and add in salt and pepper to taste.

3. In a separate deep dish combine the bread crumbs and oil together and mix until a loose mixture forms.

4. Divide the salmon mixture into 8 croquettes and add a coat of the bread crumb and oil mixture onto each.

5. Add the croquettes into the basket and insert into the Airfryer cooking the salmon croquettes for about 7 minutes. When done the croquettes should be golden brown in color.

6. Serve on a plate with a side of fresh salad and enjoy!

Chicken Wings with Chili Sauce

INGREDIENTS

2 cloves garlic

2 tsp ginger powder

1 tsp ground cumin

Freshly ground black pepper

1 lb (500 g) chicken wings at room temperature

100 ml sweet chili sauce

Directions

1. Preheat the Airfryer to 360*F (180*C).

2. Mix the following ingredients in a bowl: garlic, ginger powder, cumin, lots of freshly ground black pepper and some salt.

3. Rub the chicken wings with the herb mixture and place in the Airfryer to roast for about 10 minutes. When done the wings should be crispy and brown in color.

4. Serve on a plate with the chili sauce and enjoy as a main course or snack.

Crumbed Fish Fillets

INGREDIENTS

4 tbsp vegetable oil

3 ½ oz (100 g) breadcrumbs

1 egg

4 fish fillets

1 lemon, to serve

Directions

1. Preheat the Airfryer to 390*F (200*C).

2. Add the bread crumbs and the oil in the bowl and mix until the mixture begins to be loose and crumby.

3. In a second bowl whisk the egg and dip the fillets in or apply a coat by using a brush to paint the whisked egg on the fillets.

4. When done add the fillets in the crumb mixture covering the fillets fully.

5. Place the fillets in the Airfryer and cook for 12 minutes but be sure to monitor every now and then so that the fillets doesn't over cook or burn. Depending on the size of the fillets the time maybe more or less.

6. Serve immediately when cooked with a lemon and enjoy!

Cajun Shrimp

INGREDIENTS

1 ¼ lbs tiger shrimp (16-20 count)

¼ tsp cayenne pepper

½ tsp old bay seasoning

¼ tsp smoked paprika

Pinch of salt

1 tbsp olive oil

Directions

1. Preheat the Airfryer to 390*F (200*C).

2. Combine all the ingredients in a mixing bowl and coat the shrimp with the mixture.

3. Add the shrimp to the Airfryer and cook for about 5 minutes.

4. Serve over rice or quinoa and enjoy!

Cod Fish Nuggets

INGREDIENTS

1 lb cod, cut into strips

2 tablespoons olive oil

1 cup all-purpose flour

2 eggs, beaten

¾ cup panko breadcrumbs

1 pinch salt

Directions

1. Preheat the Airfryer to 390*F (200*C).

2. Blend the breadcrumbs, olive oil and salt in a food processor and add the fine crumb to a bowl.

3. In two separate bowls add the egg and the flour and place all 3 bowls alongside each other.

4. Coat the strips of cod first in the flour then the egg and finally the crumbs. Ensure that the crumbs are well stuck to the fish by pressing firmly into the breadcrumb mixture.

5. Add the cod nuggets to the Airfryer, shaking off any excess crumbs just before. Cook for 8 – 10 minutes or until golden brown.

6. Serve when done and enjoy!

Potato Crusted Halibut Fillets

INGREDIENTS

2 tbsp flour, all purpose enriched

1/8 tsp pepper, black freshly ground

1 egg white

1 tbsp water

¼ cup potato flakes, dehydrated

1 Fillet fish, halibut, fresh

1 tsp olive oil

Directions

1. Preheat the Airfryer to 390*F (200*C).

2. Add the flour to a shallow mixing bowl along with the black pepper.

3. In a second bowl add the egg and water and whisk to combine.

4. Grab a third bowl and add the potato flakes to it.

5. Coat the fish first in the flour mixture then the egg and finally the potato flakes.

6. Heat the olive oil over a medium high heat and place the fish in. Allow the potato crusted sides to brown then remove and add the Airfryer.

7. Cook in the Airfryer for approximately 7 minutes. When done remove, serve and enjoy!

Cornmeal Crusted Fish Sticks

INGREDIENTS

2 tbsp flour, all purpose

1/8 tsp salt, sea

1/8 tsp pepper, black freshly ground

1 1/3 tbsp cornmeal, yellow raw

¾ tsp chili powder dried

2 tbsp mayonnaise

2 ¼ tsp lemon juice

1 fillet fish, cod, atlantic, cut into 3 pieces each

Directions

1. Preheat the Airfryer to 390*F (200*C).

2. Add the flour, pepper, chili powder, cornmeal, and salt to a mixing bowl and combine.

3. Mix the mayonnaise and the lemon juice in a dish and mix the fish fillets in then into the flour mixture.

4. Add the fillets to the Airfryer and cook for approximately 5 minutes allowing the fillets to become crispy.

5. When done serve with a side dish and enjoy!

Honey Lime Chicken Wings

INGREDIENTS

16 mid joint chicken wings

2 tbsp light soya sauce

2 tbsp honey (good quality)

½ tsp sea salt

¼ tsp white pepper powder

½ tsp crush black pepper

2 tbsp lime/ lemon juice

Directions

1. Wash the wings under running water and pat dry with a kitchen towel when done.

2. Add all the ingredients from the soya sauce down to the lemon juice in a glass bowl and mix to make the marinade.

3. Add the wings to the marinade and season well in it. Let sit in the marinade for about a day. If short on time leave for 6 hours instead. Keep Covered tightly and refrigerate.

4. When done remove from the fridge and let stand for 30 minutes at room temperature before placing in the Airfryer.

5. When completed place the wings in the Airfryer at 360*F (180*C) for 15 minutes to be cooked. After the first 6 minutes flip the wings. When an additional 6 minutes goes by flip again but this time raise the heat to 390*F (200*C). Ensure that you monitor the wings carefully after the first 12 minutes has gone to prevent the chicken from burning.

6. When cooked allow the wings to cool for about 5 minutes then serve on a plate with a wedge of lime/lemon and enjoy!

Sweet and Sour Pork

INGREDIENTS

10 oz (300 g) Pork (cubed)

1 serving slice of fresh pineapple (cubed)

1 medium onion (sliced)

1 medium tomato

2 tbsp Tomato sauce

2 tbsp oyster sauce

1 tbsp worchestire sauce

Sugar (to taste)

Plain flour

1 egg

1 tbsp minced garlic

Directions

1. Begin by preparing the pork. Preheat the Airfryer to 250*F (120*C). Wait at least 5 minutes.

2. Beat the egg in a small bowl and dip the bite size cubes of pork in, coating with the egg and then covering each cube with flour.

3. Place the cubes of pork into the basket ensuring that you dust of any excess flour on the pork. Cook the pork for 20 minutes in the Airfryer.

4. When the pork is cooked prepare the sweet and sour sauce. Begin by heating a skillet on a medium high fire. Add in a tsp of oil and fry the onions and garlic.

5. When fragrant throw in the tomatoes and pineapples and cook for a few more minutes.

6. Continue by adding the next following ingredients: oyster sauce, tomato sauce and worchestire sauce. Stir the mixture.

7. After a minute or 2 add in the corn-flour and water to thicken the mixture.

8. Throw in the pieces of pork and stir the pork around in the sauce ensuring that it is well coated.

9. Finally add sugar to taste making sure that the sweetness doesn't overpower the sourness of the sauce and vice verse.

10. Let cool for a few minutes on a plate then enjoy!

Tips

- For more intense flavors marinade the pork in peppers, 2 dashes of maggi seasoning, a dash of sesame oil, and 1 tsp of light soya sauce. Cover the pork with the marinade and refrigerate for a few hours.

Skinny Crust Hawaiian Pizza

INGREDIENTS

1 tortilla wrap

1 slice of fresh pineapple

2 slices of ham

2 tbsp tomato pasta sauce

Handful of mozzarella cheese (or more if preferred)

Pinch of black pepper

Italian mixed dried herbs

Directions

1. Preheat the Airfryer to 360*F (180*C).

2. Begin by laying out the wrap on a flat surface. Evenly spread the tomato paste on the wrap and assemble the diced pineapples and ham on the top of the wrap. At this point only use about half of the pineapples and ham.

3. Drizzle the mozzarella cheese over the pineapples and ham and follow this by adding the remaining pineapples and ham.

4. Now top the wrap with the Italian herbs and sprinkle over with the black pepper.

5. Place the pizza in the Airfryer for 7 minutes and let cook.

6. When done remove and allow the pizza to cool. You can sprinkle over with some parmesan cheese if preferred and serve on a plate then enjoy!

Potatoes au Gratin

INGREDIENTS

14 oz (400 g slightly) starchy potatoes, peeled

50 ml milk

50 ml cream

Freshly ground pepper

Nutmeg

1 ½ oz (40 g) Gruyère or semi-mature cheese, grated

Directions

1. Preheat the Airfryer to 360*F (180*C).

2. Begin by thinly slicing the potatoes.

3. Combine the following ingredients in a bowl and mix well: milk, cream, and to taste salt, pepper and nutmeg. Add a coat to the potatoes when done.

4. Transfer the coated potatoes to a quiche pan arranging them evenly. Pour the milk mixture over and top with the cheese spreading evenly over the contents of the quiche pan.

5. Place the gratin in the Airfryer and bake for about 15 minutes or until nicely browned.

6. Serve with fish fillets, roast steak or any other of your choice.

Rack of Lamb

INGREDIENTS

2 racks of lamb

1 bunch fresh mint

2 garlic cloves

1/3 cup (100 ml) extra virgin olive oil

1 tbsp honey

Freshly ground pepper

Kitchen twine

Directions

1. Begin by blending the mint, honey, garlic and oil to form a thin mint pesto.

2. Preheat the Airfryer to 390*F (200*C).

3. Create a small incision from the top between the bones of the lamb racks and using a kitchen twine tie the lamb racks in the shape of a crown.

4. Coat with the mint pesto (reserve some for later) and cook in the Airfryer for 15 minutes. Every 5 minutes add another coat of the reserved pesto adding multiple layers as the rack of lamb cooks.

5. When done serve with fresh veggies of your choice and mash potatoes.

Teriyaki Steak with Hasselback Potatoes

INGREDIENTS

2 steaks, cut into strips

4 medium-sized potatoes

7 oz (200 g) snow peas, washed

8 ¾ oz (250 g) mushrooms, brushed clean and cut into quarters

1 onion, cut into half rings

Ketjap Manis sauce

Soy sauce

Olive oil

Salt and pepper

Directions

1. Add the following ingredients to a container to make the marinade: soy sauce, Ketjab Manis sauce, and olive oil. Immerse the strips of steak

in the marinade and refrigerate for a couple hours.

2. Mix all the vegetables in a bowl and drizzle with olive oil.

3. Peel the potatoes and cut a thin slice off the bottom so they are able to be well balanced on a flat surface. When done create incisions to the top cutting ¾ deep of the potatoes. Drizzle some oil in between the incisions and sprinkle over with salt and pepper.

4. Add the potatoes to the Airfryer and bake for 20 - 25 minutes at 375*F (190*F).

5. When done remove the potatoes and add in the veggies and the meat and cook for about 5 minutes at 390*F (200*C).

6. Serve them all on a plate when done and enjoy!

Mediterranean Chicken Nuggets

INGREDIENTS

2 slices stale white bread, in pieces

1 tbsp (spicy) paprika powder

8 ¾ oz (250 g) chicken fillet, in pieces

1 egg yolk + 2 egg whites

1 clove garlic, crushed

2 tbsp red pesto

Freshly ground pepper

Directions

1. Begin by adding the bread and the paprika powder to the food processor and grinding them until a crumbly mixture is formed. Add in the olive oil and mix. When done transfer to a bowl and set aside.

2. Add the chicken fillets to the food processor and puree adding in the garlic, egg yolk, pesto, and parsley. Combine with ½ tsp of salt and pepper to taste.

3. Preheat the Airfryer to 390*F (200*C).

4. Add the egg whites to a bowl and whisk. Divide the chicken mixture into 10 and roll each to form a ball. Flatten each by pressing gently on them to form the shape of the nugget.

5. Add a coat of the whisked eggs to the nuggets and dip them in the breadcrumbs right after coving all over with the crumbs.

6. Add half of the nuggets to the Airfryer and fry for about 10 minutes until the nuggets are golden brown. Do the same with the second batch.

7. When done serve with French fries or a fresh salad and enjoy!

Heated Asparagus Salad

INGREDIENTS

8 ¾ oz (250 g) white asparagus, peeled and diced

5 1/3 oz (150 g) green asparagus, peeled and diced

2 red chicory

4 boiled eggs

8 ¾ oz (250 g) small pre-boiled potatoes

8 ¾ oz (250 g) ham cubes

6 radishes, sliced

2 mandarin oranges (or 1 small tin)

7 oz (200 g) cherry tomatoes, halved

8 ¾ oz (250 g) mixed salad leaves

1 tbsp olive oil

Directions

1. Begin by adding an ovenproof dish to the Airfryer and heating it at 390*F (200*C) for 5 minutes and once heated combine the

following ingredients to the dish: olive oil, asparagus, potatoes, and ham.

2. Continue cooking at the same temperature for 10 minutes, stirring occasionally.

3. Once done let cook for a few minutes and add radishes, salad, mandarin and tomatoes to the dish.

4. Season with salt and pepper to taste and cut the chicory leaves as well as the eggs (cut into quarters).

5. Arrange nicely the chicory leaves on a large dish and add in the salad topping it with the eggs.

Saltimbocca—Veal Rolls of Sage

INGREDIENTS

1 ½ cups (400 ml) meat stock

¾ cups (200 ml) dry white wine

4 veal cutlets

Freshly ground pepper

Salt to taste

8 fresh sage leaves

4 slices cured ham

1 oz (25 g) butter

Directions

1. Preheat the Airfryer to 390*F (200*C).

2. Add the meat stock and the wine to a wide pan and bring to a boil on a medium heat. Let boil until the liquid has been reduced to 1/3 of its original amount.

3. Season the cutlets with salt and pepper and lay the sage leaves over. Roll the cutlets over and use slices of ham to wrap each cutlet. Ensure they have been firmly rolled and wrapped properly.

4. When done coat the wrapped cutlets with butter and add each to the Airfryer. Roast for 10 minutes until nicely browned and reduce the temperature to 300*F (150*C). Continue roasting for an additional 5 minutes until done.

5. Add the remaining butter to the stock and mix while seasoning with salt and pepper.

6. Slice the rolls when done and drizzle over with the gravy. Serve with a side dish and enjoy!

Broccoli and Cheese Pasta Bake

INGREDIENTS

½ tsp olive oil

½ cloves garlic, minced (1/2 tsp)

1 ½ oz pasta, penne, wholewheat (1/2 cup)

1/3 cup broccoli, cut into 1" pieces

¼ cup tomato sauce, no salt added

2 tbsp cheese, mozzarella, low sodium, grated

2 tbsp cheese, ricotta, part skim milk

1 tbsp fresh basil, chopped

½ tbsp cheese, Parmesan, low sodium, grated

1/8 tsp sea salt

1/8 tsp freshly grounded black pepper

Directions

1. Preheat the Airfryer to 360*F (180*C).

2. Add the oil to a pan over a medium heat and throw in the garlic. Cook for about a minute then set aside.

3. Place a pot of water (salted) to boil and cook the pasta in for about 9 minutes or until al dente. Add the broccoli to the pasta with 4 minutes left to cook and when done drain.

4. Meanwhile in a large bowl mix half of the mozzarella cheese as well as half of the parmesan in with the tomato sauce, ricotta, basil, and sautéed garlic.

5. Add pasta and garlic to the bowl and toss to mix. Season with salt and pepper.

6. Spoon the contents of the bowl to a 3 x 3 inch ramekin and sprinkle the remaining mozzarella and parmesan cheese over.

7. Add to the Airfryer and cook for about 8 minutes and when done let stand for a few minutes.

8. Serve and enjoy!

Salmon Quiche

INGREDIENTS

5 oz (150 g) salmon fillet, cut into small cubes

½ tbsp lemon juice

Freshly ground black pepper

3 ½ oz (100 g) flour

1 ¾ oz (50 g) cold butter, in cubes

2 eggs + 1 egg yolk

3 tbsp whipping cream

1 green onion, sliced into 1 cm pieces

Directions

1. Preheat the Airfryer to 360*F (180*C).

2. Begin by adding the salmon pieces to a bowl mixing it with the lemon juice and seasoning with salt and pepper to taste. Let the salmon rest when done.

3. In a second bowl add the flour, butter, egg yolk and ½ - 1 tbsp of cold water and mix, kneading it all to form a smooth ball.

4. Spread some flour on a working surface and roll the dough to form an 18 cm round.

5. Place the dough round in the quiche pan and spread it evenly along the edges, firmly pressing it so that it adheres to the surface. You can choose to trim the dough along the edges or allow it to roughly stick out over the edges.

6. In another mixing bowl whisk the egg, cream, mustard and salt and pepper to taste. Pour into the quiche pan and arrange the salmon pieces in. Then spread the green onions evenly over the contents of the pan.

7. Add the quiche pan to the Airfryer and cook for about 20 minutes. When done the quiche should be well done and golden brown.

8. Let cool after removing from the Airfryer then serve and enjoy!

Chapter 4

Air Fryer Desserts and Snacks Recipes

White and Dark Chocolate Brownies

INGREDIENTS

7 oz (200 g) butter

3 ½ oz (100 g) dark chocolate

3 ½ oz (100 g) white chocolate

4 small eggs

7 oz (200 g) sugar

2 tbsp of vanilla extract

3 ½ oz (100g) flour

5 oz (150 g) pecan nuts (chopped)

1 cake tin 20 x 20 cm (greased)

Directions

1. Preheat the Airfryer to 360*F (180*C).

2. In a thick-bottomed pan melt half of the butter together with the dark chocolate and leave to cool. Do the same with the white chocolate and

remaining butter in a separate pan and leave to cool as well.

3. Using a mixer beat the following ingredients together: vanilla extract, eggs and sugar.

4. Using half of the flour add in a pinch of salt. Pour in half of the sugary egg mixture and beat together until well combined. Follow by adding in the salted flour and half of the pecan nuts and mix once more.

5. Follow the same process in the previous step with the white chocolate.

6. Add the 2 chocolate mixtures side by side in the cake tin and using a spatula combine the two colors to form a swirl. Bake for 30 minutes in the Airfryer.

7. When done let cool and it's then ready to be served and enjoyed.

Stuffed Baked Apple

INGREDIENTS

2 small apples

1 tbsp raisins

Jam of your choice

2 sheets of ready-to-use puff pastry, 10 x 10 cm

2 tbsp milk

Pizza pan, 15 cm diameter

Directions

1. Preheat the Airfryer to 360*F (180*C).

2. Begin by peeling the apples and using a corer to scoop out the center of the apples. Scoop more than the usual so that the hollowed center will be large enough to be filled.

3. In a small bowl mix the jam and the raisins together.

4. Place the apples at the center of the sheets of dough and fill the hollowed apple centers with the raisin jam mixture.

5. Wrap the dough around the apple so that it is completely enclosed.

6. Place the apples onto the pan and flipping them over to have the seams facing downward. Using a brush lightly brush over the dough with the milk.

7. Place the pan into the Airfryer basket and allow the apples to cook for about 20 minutes or until it achieves a golden brown color.

8. When done let cool. Serve on a plate with vanilla ice-cream and enjoy!

Cherry Clafoutis

INGREDIENTS

7 oz (200 g) fresh cherries or 1 jar of cherries, well-drained

2-3 tbsp crème de cassis or vodka

1 ¾ oz (50 g) flour

2 tbsp sugar

1 egg

125 ml sour cream

1/3 oz (10 g) butter

Powdered sugar

Small, low cake pan, 15 cm diameter

Directions

1. Pit the cherries. This can be done by using either a straw or chopstick. Insert into the cherry and wiggle until the center of the cherry falls out. Do this over a bowl in order to catch any juices that escape the cherry.

2. When done add the cherries to a bowl and combine with the kirsch or crème de cassis.

3. In a separate bowl mix the following ingredients: four, sugar, a pinch of salt, egg and sour cream. Mix these ingredients together until a smooth, thick dough forms. A few drops of water can be added if necessary.

4. Coat the cake pan with butter and spoon some of the batter in. Evenly spread out the pitted cherries over the batter and add the remaining batter over.

5. Place the Clafoutis into the Airfryer's basket and bake for 25 minutes in the Airfryer. When done the Clafoutis should have taken on a golden brown color.

6. Right after baking is done sprinkle the Clafoutis with powdered sugar. Serve on a plate in slices and enjoy!

Chocolate Cake

INGREDIENTS

1 ¾ oz (50 g) soft butter

1 ¾ oz (50 g) fine granulated sugar

1 egg

1 ¾ oz (50 g) flour

1 tbsp cocoa

1 ¾ oz (50 g) pure chocolate, in pieces

1 small cake pan (volume 400 ml), buttered

Directions

1. Preheat the Airfryer to 320*F (160*C).

2. Mix the butter and the sugar with a mixer in a mixing bowl for about 5 minutes. The mixture should be smooth and creamy when done.

3. Beat the egg into the butter and add the following ingredients: cocoa powder, a pinch of salt and flour. Mix well and continue by adding

the grated orange peel, chocolate pieces and jam. Mix all together once more.

4. Spoon the batter into the cake pan and use a spatula to smooth out the surface of the batter.

5. Place the pan into the Airfryer's basket and bake for 25 minutes in the Airfryer. When done the cake should be nicely browned.

6. Leave the cake to cool for 5 minutes and serve in slices on a plate when done.

Tips

- To check whether the cake is ready or not when placed in the Airfryer to bake insert a tooth pick at the center of the cake and if it comes out dry then the cake is ready. If not then you know otherwise.

- For a better tasting cake make the cake one day before scheduled. Tightly wrap with clear plastic wrap and store in the fridge until when ready.

- If you're willing to try something new replace the chocolate pieces and cocoa powder with the grated peel and juice of a lemon for a lemon cake.

- For a vanilla cake replace the very same thing with the scrapings of a half pod of vanilla.

- For a chocolate ginger cake replace the chocolate pieces with 2 tbsp of candied ginger (finely chopped).

Air Fried Apple Chips

INGREDIENTS

1 apple, peeled and cored

½ tsp ground cinnamon

1 tbsp sugar

Pinch of kosher salt

Directions

1. Preheat the Airfryer to 390*F (200*C).

2. Begin by thinly slicing the apple horizontally and lay them each on a baking sheet.

3. In a bowl add and mix the other ingredients by stirring. When done sprinkle the mixture over the apple slices.

4. Place the apple slices in the basket and insert into the Airfryer to be cooked for 7 – 8 minutes and remove when done. Be sure to turn the slices over halfway through the cooking process.

5. Add the slices in a bowl and place let cool for a few minutes. When cooled enjoy!

Mini Empanadas with Chorizo

INGREDIENTS

4 ½ oz (125 g) chorizo, in small cubes

1 shallot, finely chopped

¼ red bell pepper, diced into small cubes

2 tbsp parsley

7 oz (200 g) chilled pie crust dough (pâte brisée)
or pizza dough

Olive oil

Directions

1. Drizzle some olive oil to a skillet and place on a low heat. Throw in the following ingredients to the skillet to be cooked: chorizo, chopped shallot, and bell peppers. Sauté for 2 – 3 minutes or until the bell peppers are tender.

2. Take the skillet off the heat and mix the parsley in with the contents of the skillet. Let cool after combining.

3. Preheat the Airfryer to 390*F (200*C).

4. Spread the dough over a working area and cut twenty 5 cm rounds. This can be done by using a glass to cut the dough.

5. Spoon the chorizo filling onto each round of dough and fold. Use a fork to press the edges of the dough together to seal.

6. Place half of the batch in the Airfryer and cook for about 10 minutes or until golden brown.

7. Do the same for the second batch.

8. When done serve lukewarm and enjoy!

Fried Hot Prawns with Cocktail Sauce

INGREDIENTS

1 tsp chili flakes

1 tsp chili powder

½ tsp sea salt

½ tsp freshly ground black pepper

8-12 fresh king prawns

3 tbsp mayonnaise

1 tbsp ketchup

1 tbsp cider or wine vinegar

Directions

1. Preheat the Airfryer to 360*F (180*C).

2. Begin by combining all the spices in a bowl and mixing well.

3. Coat the prawns in the spice mixture by tossing them in the bowl and place in the Airfryer to be cooked for 6 – 8 minutes. Carefully monitor to ensure that the prawns don't over cook.

4. Mix the sauce ingredients in a small bowl and serve with the prawns when cooked then enjoy!

Apricots and Rum Bread Pudding

INGREDIENTS

4 slice brioche, egg bread

Olive oil cooking spray

2 tbsp apricot preserves canned

2 tbsp raisins

1 oz apricots, dried, chopped (1/4 cup)

1 egg, large whole

¾ cup milk, low fat

½ tsp vanilla extract

½ tbsp rum, dark

Directions

6. Spread evenly the apricot preserves onto the brioche slices.

7. Spray a 5 x 5 inch ramekin with cooking spray and organize the brioche slices in the dish.

8. In a mixing bowl whisk together the egg, vanilla, ram and milk. Top the brioche slices with the raisins and apricots and pour the egg mixture over. Let the contents of the dish stand for at least 15 minutes.

9. Before that time is up preheat the Airfryer to 330*F (165*C).

10. Place the bread pudding in the Airfryer for about 10 – 12 minutes cooking until the edges of the bread darken and the bread is a lot more firm when touched.

11. Serve immediately after and enjoy!

Bake Zucchini Fries

INGREDIENTS

3 medium zucchini

2 large egg white

½ cup seasoned bread crumbs

2 tbsp grated parmesan cheese

¼ tsp garlic powder

Salt and pepper to taste

Cooking spray

Directions

1. Preheat the Airfryer to 390*F (200*C).

2. Begin by adding the eggs to a bowl with the salt and pepper and beat the ingredients together.

3. In a second bowl add the following ingredients and mix well: bread crumbs, garlic powder, and cheese.

4. Slice the zucchini into sticks and dip each into the egg mixture followed by the bread crumbs and place the breaded zucchini sticks in the Airfryer's basket.

5. Cook the zucchini in the Airfryer for 15-20 minutes or until the zucchini takes on a golden brown color.

6. When done serve with Ranch, Marinara sauce or any other dip of your choice.

Mini Frankfurters in Pastry

INGREDIENTS

1 tin of mini frankfurters (drained weight 7 oz/220 g, approx. 20 frankfurters)

3 ½ oz (100 g) ready-made puff pastry (chilled or frozen, defrosted)

1 tbsp fine mustard

Directions

1. Preheat the Airfryer to 390*F (200*C).

2. Begin by cutting the puff pastry into strips measuring 5 x 1 ½ cm.

3. Add a thin coat of mustard to each strip and roll each sausage spirally into a strip of pastry.

4. When done add half of the pastry rolled sausages in the Airfryer and cook for about 10 minutes or until they become golden brown. Do the same with the other batch.

5. Serve with a side of mustard or any other dip you choose and enjoy!

Buttermilk Blueberry Banana Bread

INGREDIENTS

1 ¾ cups all-purpose flour

1 tsp baking powder

1/8 tsp baking soda

¼ tsp salt

½ cup unsalted butter, at room temperature

1 cup sugar

2 large eggs

¼ cup buttermilk

½ tsp vanilla extract

3 ripe bananas

1 cup blueberries

Directions

1. Preheat the Airfryer to 360*F (180*C).

2. Spray a light layer of non-stick spray in four 5 ¾ inch mini loaf pans.

3. Combine the following ingredients in a large bowl: baking powder, flour, salt and baking soda.

4. Using an electric mixer beat butter and sugar together until light and fluffy. This can be done by placing the mixer on medium high for 2-3 minutes.

5. When done add in the buttermilk, eggs and vanilla to the mixing bowl and beat until well combined.

6. While the contents of the bowl are being beaten mash the bananas together and add it to the mixing bowl and beat until well combined.

7. Reduce the speed of the electric mixer to low and add flour gradually to the bowl just until the ingredients are almost incorporated.

8. Throw in the blueberries and gently toss to combine.

9. Place the loaf pans side by side to each other and spoon/scoop the batter into each pan, evenly separating the batter.

10. Place the pan into the basket of the Airfryer and bake for 30-35 minutes or until an inserted toothpick comes out clean.

11. When ready remove from the Airfryer and let cool for 10-15 minutes.

12. When cooled slice, serve and enjoy!

Molten Lava Cakes

INGREDIENTS

1 ½ tbsp self rising flour

3 ½ tbsp baker's sugar (not powdered)

3 ½ oz (100 g) unsalted butter

3 ½ oz (100 g) dark chocolate (pieces or chopped)

2 eggs

Directions

1. Preheat the Airfryer to 390*F (200*C).

2. Payout 4 standard oven safe ramekins side by side. Grease and flour each and set aside.

3. Add the butter and dark chocolate to a microwave safe bowl and melt in the microwave for 3 minutes at level 7. Stir throughout during this process.

4. When done remove and stir once more until the mixture is consistent.

5. Add the eggs and sugar to a bowl and beat until the mixture is frothy and pale.

6. When complete pour the chocolate and butter mixture into the bowl with the egg and stir. Add in the flour and continue mixing until there's an even consistency.

7. Pour the mixture into the ramekins filling each to about ¾ of the ramekins. Place in the basket of the Airfryer and bake for 10 minutes in the preheated Airfryer.

8. When done remove from the Airfryer and let it stand for a couple minutes to cool then serve it on a plate by placing it upside down over the plate and tapping it lightly in order for the cakes to slide out. Serve with berries and enjoy!

Chapter 4: What to Consider When Buying an Airfryer

Capacity

Taking into consideration what it is you're going to cook in your Airfryer on a daily basis is very important and close attention must be paid to the type of Airfryer in relation to this. Why? Allow me to answer this with another question. Would you really like to be cooking the same meal in batches? It's because of this you will need to pay attention to how much food the Airfryer you're opting to buy will be able to hold. In general, Airfryers are capable of holding between 1.5 pounds – 2.5 pounds of food. This is very reasonable for cooking what is considered to be the "regular" meal such as fries, drumsticks, etc, but if you're looking to cook an entire turkey the amount of weight the Airfryer can hold must be increased. Assess what exactly you want to be cooking in your Airfryer and make a purchase that will fulfill those needs.

Wattage

This may not have been on your checklist on things to consider when purchasing you're an Airfryer but it's more important than you think. Ensure that the electrical outlets that are at your home can supply enough wattage for proper functioning of the Airfryer. Air fryers typically need a wattage ranging from 800 – 1400 watts in order to perform and provide satisfactory results. Checking the exact amount of power needed for the Airfryer you're considering to buy and whether or not it falls in the range of the supply at home might just prevent an unfortunate situation.

Size/Space

Airfryers are appliances that sometime take up a lot of counter space and no one wants to purchase any appliance that can't be placed properly in the area that you want. When picking an Airfryer keep in mind how much space is available so that when the Airfryer is placed in its location it won't stand out as much but rather complement the aesthetic appeal of the surrounding area.

Settings

It's obvious that not all Airfryers come with the same settings and the range of settings that a particular Airfryer comes with might be more favorable to you based on the meals that are to be prepared in the Airfryer. What do I mean by this? Depending on the meals that are going to be prepared in the Airfryer higher temperatures may be required and opting for an Airfryer that has those particular setting will prove to be a better purchase. Once again I advise you to make a careful assessment of what is required for the foods that are to be prepared in the Airfryer.

Additional Features

With the range of Airfryers that are out there customers are drawn to certain features due to the fact that it might be more beneficial to them. The different features that are available now make it easy to find one that suits your personal preference such as digital programmable settings, oil free fryers, rapid cook technology and so much more. The challenge now is to find what works best for you that will fit in just right.

Pricing

Last but not least, the price. The price that you pay for something is all too important and although there are individuals who focus more on the quality of the product there are those too who focus on the amount that is paid. In both cases each individual most times has good reason for their determining factor with respect to pricing but one should not expect to get a high quality Airfryer at an average price. It's not surprising to see an Airfryer priced above the $200 mark but customers who have paid such and even more has testified that the Airfryer purchased provided way more value than what was paid for. But if you're looking for an Airfryer to do the basics and be good at that then you will still be able to get one at a reasonable price.

Top 5 Best Airfryers

Even when you know what to look for in a product it can still be a stressful and frustrating experiencing when you're entirely new to it all. Being able to differentiate the bad from the good and the good from the best is a skill that may take some time to develop. Thankfully we decided to take away that uncertainty when differentiating the different Airfryers by providing a list of our top 5. The Airfryers that are going to be mentioned have proved to be the best of the best and have shown their value with every purchase made.

Philips HD9230/26 Digital AirFryer

- Uses very little oil (70% reduction in fat)
- Features a double layer rack
- Holds up to 1.8 pounds of food
- Cooks food quickly
- Uses a wattage of 1,425
- Great food quality based on customers feedback

T-fal FZ700251 ActiFry

- Has a large food capacity. Holds up to 2.2 pounds of food
- Easily cooks multiple servings at once

- Uses a wattage of 1,450

GoWISE USA GW22621 4th Generation Electric Air Fryer

- Temperature range of 360*F (180*C) to 390*F (200*C).
- Fits nicely on kitchen counters
- Does up to 30 minutes of cooking

Air Fryer with Digital Programmable Settings by Good Cooking

- Provides a 2.5 quartz capacity
- Uses a wattage of 1,200
- Particularly does well with meats based on customers feedback

Kalorik Convection Air Fryer

- Has a large cooking capacity of 4.2 quartz
- Uses a wattage of 1,230

Conclusion

Once more I would like to thank you for purchasing this book but also for reading it through.

There's no doubt that exercising the use of an Airfryer will provide massive benefits to you and your family and this is why I believe that creating this book was so important. How amazing is it to be eating your favorite fried foods with that much less fat? Too amazing I would say so I hope that this book was able to provide enough value to you and allowed you to enjoy deliciously healthy meals using this game changing product. I wish you the best of luck on your journey to a healthier lifestyle!

Made in the USA
Lexington, KY
06 April 2016